Thank you to all the amazing mummies who contributed a poem to this book.

This book is dedicated to my mother, without whom I would be nothing.

Lots of love
Corinna xxx

So Much

So much love
Overpowering overwhelming love
So much loneliness
Overpowering overwhelming loneliness

So much pain
Hopeless hurting harm
So much laughter
Healing hopeful happiness

So much.

Sue Nicol

About birth...

You came into my life...
Was it the Autumn of 2018?
In the bathroom with harsh light
You were a strong double line

Every night you'd say hello
You tickled me with your feet at 3 or 4
I tried to imagine your face
Or anything about your looks
There was only dark soft space
And our bond

I wanted to protect you
From strangers' touch
From the world at large
I tried to push calmly, gently
When you appeared earthside
Your father caught you underwater
With a steady hand

They said I gave birth to you
But what they failed to see
Was that it was you who birthed a new me

Magdalena Finn

They Said

The moment we went from
One to two
They said I had to
Put You Down

My heart said up
But it seemed to be important
That I
Put You Down

Something about
rods and backs.

They said you would
Spoil
As though you were a piece of fruit

You are not a piece of fruit
My darling
You are the whole universe
Curled small on my chest

Who could put the universe down?

They didn't say anything about that.

Stacey Harrower

Rainbow Baby

From the moment you were a seed in my belly,
Was a feeling that turned my legs into jelly,
I saw the world through different eyes,
and what was to come took me by total surprise,
From the moment that you were placed on my chest,
The feeling was unreal and quite simply the best,
I kissed your head and your tiny little toes,
and looked into your eyes and at your button nose
Each day I watch as you grow and you grow,
And you surprise me each day
With how much you know.
My rainbow baby sent to me from above,
I feel truly blessed and feel the deepest of love.
You see my dear son you mean the world to me,
And I cannot wait to see who you turn out to be.

To my gorgeous Jack, Love from mummy x

Nicola Fenton

My Angel

An angel sent from heaven,
when all hope had been lost
You have my heart forever,
I'll protect you at all costs
In my arms I carry you,
but you always lead the way
A little giggle or a smile,
every time we go astray
We're learning as we go,
looking for every subtle cue
I've quickly come to realise,
that all I need is you
Everyday is a new adventure,
starring you and me
For now until eternity,
my angel you'll always be

Laura Lewis

You and I

I'm still amazed at how far we've come
Day after day, a mother and her son
From tiny toes, to your cute button nose
A love so strong, only a mother knows
You're the only one who's heard my heart
From the inside, a work of art
My blood, your blood through our veins
Your face of wonder, when it rains
I watch you sleep, a smile on your face
The wonder of you, never ceases to amaze
My love, you came and stole my heart
The strongest bond, even when we're apart.

Laura Lewis

Superhuman

You scream at the world as you enter it.
Your voice attacks our ears and punches the
stunned silence.
Angry. Afraid. Mottled,
Your elastic skin- wrinkled and resilient- is a
smudge of blue and purple. Non-human.
A white glaze protects you from the new world
as you bungee from a dark rope that ties us
together.

Your senses amaze us.

You know who we are and what to do.
You suckle, eager to grow and sustain.
My body fails. Cracks. Bleeds. I'm Bruised.
Powerless.

Infantile night vision scans the new territory as I
battle to keep my eyes open,
your body restless and fighting.
Tiny fists jab stale air, punching away invisible
sleep that is your enemy- and my friend.
Red faced and swollen, my dear, you squeal.
I rest my breast in your mouth and release my
power.
And we are superhuman together

Sadie Smyth

This poem was written for Clare Clifford and read out at her daughter's funeral when she died suddenly at 7.5 month old (SIDS).

Imagine every face you ever see is smiling at you,
The eyes behind the smiles are full of love and the noises you hear are warm and happy,
You can't know what they mean but you can't help but know they are just for you.
Imagine being the centre of a complete Universe,
It's all about you and that's how it's meant to be for now,
The time and effort and love is unconditional...
You can bathe in the glow of such adoration,
Nothing is ever going to be expected of you.
Imagine every discomfort, need, frustration or desire
Being tended to by caring loving giants...
You can't reason or rationalise it right now but you can feel...that's how it's meant to be, it's cool, this is my life now,
That's why your biggest smiles are for the three giants who are there all the time.
Imagine your last moments on earth, deep in the womb of love that is your family home,
Curled up next to someone who really just couldn't love you more than she does, nobody could...
Imagine passing from this world surrounded by love and care without a tinge of worry or fear, totally wrapped in love.
It's not a dream, that's the lovely world you created for Charlotte,
Not every child gets to be lucky enough to have you two for a Mum and Dad.

Written by Anthony Brown, read as part of Charlotte's eulogy.

<u>A Little Too Soon</u>

It wasn't supposed to be like this
We had so many weeks to go
No birth plan, no nursery, no car seat
No instagrammable baby grow,
All the excitement and anticipation
Has turned to worry and fear
I can't believe you gatecrashed week 30
I can't believe you're already here.

Every morning now starts with a doctors round
Nurses dressed in shades of blue,
They huddle round space-age equipment
And give an update on you.
I'll listen in very closely
As I look down at your perspex cocoon,
You're here and you're stable
You just came a little too soon.

The bradys, the desats, the apnea
All these words all new to me
So I'll go on Dr Google
Like I'm studying for a medical degree
Of course I'll scare myself stupid
With what the results will show,
Then I remember you're here and healthy
You just need some more time to grow.

Sharing those precious moments
Wondering if it's wind or a smile,
Changing nappies through little doors
Like it's a bush tucker trial.
The sadness of leaving you each night
Before bed, the ward I would call,
The nurses say he's here and he's thriving
He's just a little too small.

Every day you're getting stronger
Another milestone off the list
Out comes the feeding tube
Our first cuddle, our first kiss
No more scary incubator,
as we move rooms up the hall
You're making such great progress
You just wanted to see us all.

At last we place you in your car seat
Off to home we go!
You just needed time to get stronger
You just needed time to grow
And as we reach the front door
We say softly in your ear
We're so very proud of you
and so glad that you are here.

Claire Pace

I AM Enough

I am enough,
I am your everything,
Your eyes light up,
When you hear me sing.

You're my tiny miracle,
I love you so much.
Perfect little features,
Skin so soft to touch.

I never knew,
How strong love can be,
But now I've got you,
It's so clear to see.

This love is fierce,
I've never felt it before,
I watch you sleep,
I want to cuddle you some more.

I am your world,
And you are mine,
We've had a long day though,
Now pass me the wine.

Emily Hodson.

Every day I'll try my best

As I see you sound asleep
I look at you with pride
How did I manage to create such perfection
That darling twinkle in your eye
I heard of mother's love before
But nothing could ever comprehend
The moment they showed me your face
My suffering came to an end.
When I heard no crying,
Fear took over me,
What was happening to my baby
And where could he possibly be?
When they said they had to resuscitate
The heartache was overwhelming
They put you on my chest, alive,
And the medical staff were outstanding
And there you were,
My baby boy as healthy as can be
My heart was empty, missing a piece
Until the universe sent you to me.
I may not always get it right
And sometimes need a rest
But I promise you my baby,
Every day I'll try my best

Kirsten Clark

Learning to bond

People say "that overwhelming rush of love,
you feel it in an instant"
My baby was out now,
so why did I feel so distant?

In the hospital, after giving birth,
you're offered tea and toast
People had told me about this moment,
it's supposedly loved the most

But my tea was rubbish
and my toast was flappy
What's wrong with me?
Why am I not happy?

People ask "I'd like to hold him,
is that OK?"
Well he's not in my arms,
so "fill your boots" I'd say

I daren't say anything to anyone,
I was already failing to be a decent Mum
Don't get me wrong, I do love my son,
but it wasn't how everyone said it would be and these
thoughts weren't much fun

But as each day goes by,
our bond and love grows
And I started to really notice
your perfect button nose

A bit of mid-night reading
and it turns out I'm not alone.
I thought maybe I can fix this,
and without picking up the phone

I did some more research
and it appears to not be my fault,
I feel ready now,
to talk to others and unlock my vault

The stress of pregnancy
and all those hormones,
Those aches and pains,
my body still groans

My labour and your delivery
were a huge disaster,
And thanks to surgery,
I was basically one big plaster

We were both very poorly
and for days needed monitoring,
It was just me on a night,
why weren't you sleeping?

Exhausted and upset
and desperate to be home,
I had a beautiful baby
and I felt I had no right to moan

Reflection is important,
to release all that guilt.
I did what I could at the time
and now our love is built.

Hayley Hawthorne

<u>Unexpected joy</u>

I thought I'd never have you,
For years I was told,
A dream upon a dream
For one I would be sold.

I moved to a different country,
Starting my life anew,
I started to feel unwell,
Ignoring it I pushed through.

I finally went to a doctor,
And with a smile she looked at me,
Congratulations, is what I heard,
I felt shocked, scared and giddy.

The day you came into the world,
Me a mum, who knew?
My missing piece was finally filled,
The day that I had you.

Kirsten Clark.

Miracles

I believe in miracles
Ask me about mine.
29 weeks in, the thought of you divine.
But your map had a different route
Cut from my body- I watched on, mute.
Machines did what I failed to do,
I sat, baited breath, believing in you.
The Lord above gave me twins,
but your introduction to the world made me
recount and repent all my sins.
Now you are two, and I'm sure I'm owed a
lifetime of sleep in lieu!
You are perfect in every single way
and I think what I'm trying to say,
is that my darling twins I will forever more
keep you out of harm's reach
Each and every day.

Love always your mummy x

Kimberley Virr

Let's make a baby

Let's make a baby, we said, said we
And thus began the start of our story
Anticipation, excitement through and through
Our own little family is a dream come true

But then a year passes us slowly by
As each month goes on, we try and try
Now apprehension seeps into our life
I wanted to be something more than a wife

Time moves forward, another year on
And still no second line to gaze upon
Medical appointments have both of us offended
Has our dream of a family really ended?

One day, after too many sticks and charts
And numerous doctors breaking our hearts
Suddenly a second line out of the blue
Our amazement and wonder – is it true?

No sir, this one was not meant to be
The grief held strong, my heart empty
The cycle of pain made stronger and stronger
Can we keep going like this for much longer?

Never fear - one day, it will work out
Was advice we would get when others were about
We were still wondering if this was true
When all of a sudden another second line of blue

Nine months later, imagine our joy
When into the world we welcome a baby boy
Never have I felt a love so strong
It wiped away all that went wrong

The struggle we felt for almost three years
The stress, the disappointment, all the tears
Yet I can't even remember how it felt before
Because each day I fall in love more and more

Louise Ericsson

Book Club

I want to show you Hogwarts
and let magic fill your head.
Take you to Willy Wonka's
and eat candy before bed.

Let's find out the wardrobe's secrets,
meet Mr Tumnus too.
What happened to Cinderella,
how did she lose that shoe?

We'll fall down the hole with Alice,
join the Mad Hatter there.
I've heard about a giant peach
that can fly through the air.

Shall we visit The Shire,
where the friendly Hobbits live?
Lie in wait for the BFG,
he has lots of dreams to give.

Soon we will climb the Faraway Tree,
see Moon-Face on the way.
Let's find the secret garden,
we can play there night and day.

I want to show you everything,
let magic fill your head,
Take you on adventures
until you head right off to bed.

Liv Young

This time last week

This time last week your little sister was born
And during those seven days,
Everything has felt new to me,
My heart has felt quite torn.
Between breastfeeding or your stickers,
Newborn cuddles or your bike,
I want to be with you both,
But try as I might...
You need very different parts of me,
Your sister needs my body,
But you need my time and attention,
And for this I wasn't ready.
You haven't seemed to notice,
Mummy's latest struggle,
And that's because you're 2 years old,
And you're happily living in your bubble.
But if and when you pick it up,
That mummy's time is torn,
I need you to know that with every breath,
I love you,
My first born.

Lauren Todd
(Laurella Mama)

<u>Making Mother</u>

I look at you so sweet in sleep,
Where I've placed my heart to keep,
Amazed that I could love this much,
Amazed by every single touch,
Such depth of feeling for another,
All for you, who's made me Mother.

But can I help you grow and thrive,
When I'm still learning what's inside,
Discovering what Mother means,
Uncovering the instincts in my genes,
And who I am in this new guise,
This new part of which I now comprise.

Some days the load is just so heavy,
Some days the weight too much for me,
How can I give you all you need,
And set you up to best succeed,
This job I have is so extremely tough,
How can I, ME, be enough?

Yet with each and every cry placated,
Each sunshine smile for which I've waited,
Each burst of pride for a milestone reached,
Each gurgled sound that you've screeched,
You forge me into something new,
You make me feel a Mother true.

Lexi Hurt

Sleep thief

I birthed you into this world of ours
And here you are to stay
I long to watch you sleeping endless hours
But it appears you much prefer to play!

I aim to teach you wrong from right
And hope to raise you well
You do not yet "sleep through the night"
I'm sure from my eye-bags that all can tell!

Not to worry, this tired Mama don't mind
There's plenty more time for bed
A bond and love like ours is hard to find
And just think of the fun times ahead!

You're learning how to walk and move
Growing up right before my eyes
We've finally got into our own little groove
There has already been so many highs!

You'll always be my partner in crime
These memories, I'll make sure to keep
Nothing will come between your heart and mine
But I just wish you would go to bloody sleep!!

Debs Hastings

A mother I was made to be

I always knew, as far back as I can remember,
Inside me was this burning ember.

A mother I was made to be,
But was I ready for this journey?

For me the road was a long one,
A chapter I had just begun.

Four before you were there, sweet girl
Every one a precious little pearl.

They were sent to me, but not meant for this earth,
To them I would never give birth.

They changed my life in ways I didn't expect,
Time I needed to reflect.

I began to believe it was not meant to be,
A wish, a desire that I had set free.

But then my darling, along came you,
I couldn't believe it was really true.

Twelve weeks passed, Sixteen then Twenty,
Did I dare to believe this was meant to be?

Finally precious girl you made your way,
I will never ever forget the day.

I treasure every moment with you, for you make
me complete,
A babe I thought I would never meet.

When you're old enough to understand,
I'll sit beside you and hold your hand.

As I tell you about your siblings above,
How they watch over you and I with love.

Our shining stars in the night sky,
A mother I was made to be.

Charli England

Mommy's Alright

I know I may not seem alright darling and though
I will always be your mummy,
I can't always smile, hold you tightly
cook you food that's yummy.
I know I may seem odd sometimes
and perhaps angry, distant or sad,
but know this, my precious babe,
you have not been naughty or bad.
It is not because of you
that I sometimes feel this way,
and there's nothing you can do
or that anyone can say.
I promise it isn't forever
that mummy will feel unhappy and blue.
And I swear more than anything
that it's not because of you.
I love you so very much,
so much it makes me hurt inside my tummy,
that this illness might affect you
and sometimes takes away your mummy.
I'd give everything I have
and all my soul I would invest,
if I didn't have to have this thing;
didn't have to be depressed.
but, my shining diamond light,
oh sweet baby of mine,
today I may not be okay
or tomorrow not be fine.
But I have you darling,
and there is no if; or maybe;
that you are my earth, and sun,
and stars and moon,

my sweet, beloved, baby.
I choose you and I will keep choosing you,
every single time,
Because of you Mommy
will at least always be just fine.
The best I can say right now
is that mom's a little broken,
But I'm holding myself together
with feelings and words unspoken.
And I will be ok, even if it's only for you.
You will be my fixing tape,
staples, nails and glue.
Wherever I am, wherever you are – my love will
never be just pending,
This is just part of our story my dear
and is certainly not the ending.

Joelle Byrne

Toddlers

Mummy!
Mummy, mummy, it's time to get up!
Mummy, mummy, I built a tower, have a look!
Mummy, mummy, I did a wee on the floor
Mummy, mummy, please open the door
Mummy, mummy, I need another snack,
Mummy, mummy, when will you be back?
Mummy, mummy, are you going to the loo?
Mummy, mummy, wait for me, I want to come too!
Mummy, mummy, I feel sad
Mummy, mummy, I'm sorry, I didn't mean to be bad
Mummy, mummy, can you come and play?
Mummy, mummy, I want to build a den today!
Mummy, mummy can we look at this book?
Mummy, mummy, where is my blue truck?
Mummy, mummy, can you tuck me in nice and tight?
Mummy, mummy, just one more kiss before you turn
out the light
Mummy, mummy, what else can we do?
Mummy, mummy, I really love you!

Helen Handlovics

Love You Mummy

I wake in the morning with you beside me in bed
With your feet tickling me in the head
We rush to get ready for nursery and work
You dither about and talk back with a smirk
You want to feed yourself your breakfast,
and put on your own shoes?!
We don't have time for this,
no you can't refuse!
Get in the car, quick we're late!
Oh you want to try and strap yourself in, great!
You want to listen to twinkle twinkle little star
again?
I'm fed up of arguing, okay then!
We pull up at the door, 15 minutes late
Your hair looks an absolute state
I run behind you, trying to put in a bobble
You scream like I'm being completely immoral
As I hand you over at the door,
ready to play in nursery bliss
You say, 'love you mummy'
and blow me a kiss
I get in the car and breathe a sigh
I promise myself
tomorrow morning will be easier,
and try not to cry.

Lucy Whitehead-Alofi

You will always be our precious, favourite 'What if?'

Today should have been a very exciting day
But it's so different to how we had planned,
We should have been in that room now, waiting to
see you on that screen,
Daddy anxiously holding Mummy's hand.

Instead today we will think of you,
As we do of course every other day,
We love you baby boy or girl,
How we wish you would have been here to stay.

We don't get to share our news with the world
After seeing beautiful you on the scan,
It's all just so cruel and the pain is still there,
All this wasn't part of our plan.

Jay still plays with the teddy you gave him,
A part of you will always be here,
If you see Mummy cry, don't worry,
I can't help but feel sad sometimes and need to shed
a little tear.

I now need to focus on the time that I got with you
As that I will always be grateful for,
I may not have been able to hold you in my arms
But compared to some people I got so much more.

I got to keep you with me, tucked up and warm
And you kept me warm too,
You got to know a little more about me
And I feel I got to know so much about you.

Our precious second baby,
You'd have been a beauty like your bro for sure,
You'd have loved your cheeky big brother, he'd have
wound you up and teased you

But what are big brothers for?

Jay has always been our absolute world
And I used to think I'd find it hard to share my love
between two,
Now I know about you and have you though,
I know it's absolutely something I could do.

For the love I have doesn't need to be shared,
It simply doubles and I have plenty,
You're our little baby Jackson number two,
'Should have' been with us in December 2020

Sammi Jackson

Twinkle Twinkle my little child

Twinkle twinkle my little child
I love you, though you're a little wild

You chip my cups and break my plates
Delicate wines glasses have met their fate
I dread those words at a family do
'I think somebody's had a poo'

My hair was thick with a glowing shine
Now it's dry, frizzy and fine
I used to bathe for many an hour
Now I'm lucky for a 3 minute shower

I drank fancy bubbles and expensive wine
Exclusive restaurants, fine food to dine
Now it's soft play and play dates
With luke warm coffee and sweet cakes

My sexy underwear was lacy and silk
It's now grey cotton and smells of milk
My shoes were high, my clothes were new
Now they're baggy and covered in spew

BUT

My heart sings when you laugh and smile
You're the most beautiful thing by a country mile
And when you're all grown up and no longer need me
I hope you meet someone who sees what I see.

Hayley Marsh

Becoming

The first cry
The first touch
The first embrace

You are finally here!
I wish I could hold you forever.

Pavlina Papadopoulou

Born in lockdown: a poem for my daughter

On Monday 23rd of March,
One month 'til you were due,
The country's lockdown was announced,
For how long nobody knew.

Anxiety overwhelmed me,
The urge to keep you safe,
I stayed at home protecting you
And tried not to lose faith.

As sunny garden days went by,
Your arrival ever nearer,
I longed for you to stay inside(!)
For things to all be clearer.

Packing my bag, I questioned
How I'd cope once you were here.
How long would Daddy get to stay,
To bond, to hold you near?

A month "just us" in isolation
And then our bubble burst!
You started coming, blue lights to hospital-
Not how we'd rehearsed!

The relief that flowed with 'gas and air',
The midwife's calming tones -
From behind her mask she reassured,
I cast away unknowns.

An hour later you were here –
Healthy, pink, and loud!
The look of love on Daddy's face,
A beaming smile - so proud.

On the screen you met your family,
A shining ray of light.
The "can't wait to meet you's" loaded with sadness,
No end of lockdown in sight.

Back home to your brother,
Eagerly waiting for Mummy and Daddy's return.
Told of a baby - he'd no understanding,
How life would change - he'd soon learn!

You'll never know the joy you've brought us,
Until you have your own.
For now be little, be with me, and needing
... Until you're fully grown

Marguerite Waters

Mummy Pains

Breakfast, snack time, lunchtime,
snack time, teatime, bed.
The gaps between mealtimes are tiny,
It's tricky keeping you fed.

Washing, drying, mopping,
Cleaning, tidying & vac
I literally don't have time to think,
Mess each time I turn my back

Painting, baking, crafting,
Football, trampoline, pool
It's a full time job keeping you busy,
(I'll be bored when you're at school)

iPads, YouTube, games
videos, shows, TV
They can be such a blessing at times,
Like when I need a hot tea.

It feels like it's never ending,
It feels like I'll never win,
The mess, the noise, the arguing,
It's going to seriously do me in.

And then, you come and find me,
usually when I'm on the loo,
and all of the stresses disappear,
when you whisper, "Mummy, I WUV you"

Sian Pearson

I'm an addict

New human
You are so beautiful
New human
I love You so much

New life
You're so tiring
Like any other baby
You puke and poo
Just when I put brand new clothes on You

New life, You surprise me
You're competent
You know so much
You know how to live a good life

New life, Your smell is amazing
I'm grateful You taught me how and
You taught me why
New life,
Thank You for daily oxytocin high

Magdalena Finn

Birth Trauma Baby

Birth Trauma baby
Do I love you today?
It's taken so long
But it will be ok.

They said, "but he's worth it",
I nodded and sighed.
How can he be worth
All this pain trapped inside?

I failed, I failed and
My punishment is
I can't feel a thing with
Each cuddle and kiss.

Birth Trauma baby
Can I love you today?
Have I been good enough?
What would you say?

That warmth and that joy
That the other mums boast
It sounds just so easy
That's what hurts the most.

Birth Trauma baby
Should I love you today?
It's been a long time now
But it's still far away.

I can feel it getting closer
But I've been here before
It just turned around
And walked out of the door

Somehow this time's different
They've all said it's there
Just because I can't feel it
Doesn't mean I don't care.

Like a child with a wish
I close my eyes tight.
Will it be there in the morning?
I'm hoping it might.

Birth Trauma baby
I can love you today
I'm doing my best
And that's the way it will stay.

I'm looking at my baby
He's sleeping
I let myself love him.
I'm allowed to, I deserve it, I want it, I need it.

I'm doing it, I did it, I made him and bore him and
birthed him and held him and fed him and
cleaned him and taught him and rocked him and
drove him and pushed him and kept him,
Over and over and all this time because,
I love him.

Sheryl Wynne

Matresence

Oh matresence -
What I wouldn't give to have known about you
Before becoming a mummy to my precious
baby girl Sophia.

Halida Danby

That cute little...

Intermittent sleeping and waking in the night,
That cute little smile, that just makes it all alright.
Screaming as you lay him down on your lap,
That cute little hand on your chest as they nap.
A headache from no sleep and no food,
That cute little giggle
that takes away your rotten mood.
Poo that squelches right up past his shoulder,
That cute little photograph you take
to laugh when he's older.
That tune from a toy that plays over and over,
That cute little noise he makes
that makes you not bothered.
Toys and clutter all over the floors.
That cute little action that makes you buy more.
Life is different with a baby in your life.
That cute little human is worth every tiny strife.

Laura Holdsworth

<u>Laying here in the dark</u>

Laying here in the dark
The comforting warmth of you next to me
The gentle sound of your breathing
Your sweet smell, so familiar
Overwhelming love washing over me
As we drift off to sleep

Laying here in the dark
No covers, on the edge of the bed
The low rumble of your snoring
Your sweaty little hand on my face
Overwhelming love washing over me
But maybe not much sleep

Rebecca Blake

Worship the Goddesses Out There!

Interrupted Sleep.
Relentless.
Tiredness.
Relentless.
Clutter.
Relentless.
Laundry.
Relentless.
Tidying up.
Relentless.
Guilt.
Relentless.
Chasing my tail.
Relentless.
Nobody. Even. Cares.
Overwhelm.
I know the true meaning of *sisyphean.*

He complains- he can't finish his sandwich.
He had a 3 hour lie-in.
My coffee goes cold,
3 times before I've a chance
to heat it up again.

Then I look at your downy hair,
I sniff your soft skin,
and I melt.

Welcome to Motherhood.
Daily heaven and hell.

Mothers need worship as well.

Magdalena Finn

Motherhood

The test read pregnant 1-2 weeks
I started to smile, it hurt both cheeks.

The weeks seemed to fly by, and drag as well
Pregnancy- now that was a new kind of hell.

I loved my bump and seeing my boys
But pregnancy for me was not all joys.

And then you came into our world
Born in water and into my body you curled.

I held you close, we had skin to skin
My life had completely changed I knew right then.

I'd never felt a love for another like this
Holding you close felt like such bliss.

The weeks fly by and my baby just grew
Every single moment I loved him… even if I did drink
a cold brew.

He's growing up so quickly, everything I miss
But some days I just cuddle him and he gives
mummy a kiss.

Elizabeth Wood

Homebirth

Affirmations all around,
My own towels on the ground,
And my favourite candles burning out their scents.
My babies' pictures on display,
With another making way,
It truly is something heaven sent.

Remembering my breathing,
Riding surges all the time.
The waves are doing wonders
Nearing the distance between this child of mine.

As she crowns and holds her stay,
And I rest and breathe away,
I realise she's here.
For this child I did pray.

She floats into my arms,
It's silent and she's so calm.
We stare for an age.
We know this family story has gained a page.

Teresa Newsome

Big Boy Shoes

Today I bought big boy shoes
Big shoes to fill, of course he will,
And make his own path, journey, plans and dreams
Through gritted teeth and silent screams
I'll watch and let him learn,
And kiss the burns of fingers
My big boy, still so very small.

Carol Barwick

<u>My World</u>

It's a dark and lonely world
But you are here.
The nights are long and cold
But you are here.
My world is large and yet so small
But you are here.
Sometimes I feel abandoned
But you are here.

I know you feel lost mummy,
So do I
I know you feel scared,
So do I
I know you feel overwhelmed,
So do I
I know you need love,
So do I

As we cuddle together
My baby
Your smile fills my heart
My baby
Stronger than I have ever been
My baby
Indescribable love

Lois Jowett

<u>Little do they know</u>

They have only disdain for you
You don't conform
Although you're the norm

You don't fit their narrow
erased, airbrushed, shallow
You're not insta-ready

Some see right through you
Like through a ghost that has given up what they love
most...
Themselves

They pity your tired eyes and your less than flat belly
Completely unaware
Of the power you hold

They haven't seen you
Conjuring a new being
Whilst running on a treadmill
Or chairing a meeting
And growing that beauty

They will never conceive how
You owned being split in two
You roared out such perfection
My body, I love you!

My body, you know...
We are women
We give birth to the entire world!

Magdalena Finn

Useful Links of organisations

The Mummy Circle
Community, love and support for the first year of your baby's life and beyond. Online membership, virtual Baby Massage classes, and much more.
https://themummycircle.com
https://www.facebook.com/themummycircle

AIMS
AIMS works towards better births for all, by campaigning and information sharing, protecting human rights in childbirth and helping women to know their rights, whatever birth they want.
https://www.aims.org.uk

Birthrights
Birthrights promotes women's rights to receive evidence-based care that conforms to the best medical and midwifery standards. They do not promote any particular clinical perspectives in maternity care.
www.birthrights.org.uk

Bliss
If you've had a premature or sick baby, Bliss have information to support you. They offer emotional and practical support to empower families and equip them with the knowledge and skills they need to provide the best possible care for their baby.
https://www.bliss.org.uk

Home Birth Support Group UK
A doula facilitated, peer to peer support group. The group is UK based. All members have an interest in or are planning a home birth. (Facebook private group.)

Kicks Count
Advice on empowering women to monitor their babies' movements during pregnancy.
https://www.kickscount.org.uk

The Lullaby Trust
Information and support on safer sleep.
https://www.lullabytrust.org.uk

La Leche League
Breastfeeding support
https://www.laleche.org.uk

Traumatic Birth Recovery
Support for families recovering from a traumatic birth.
https://www.traumaticbirthrecovery.com

Tamba
Support for families with twins, triplets and more
https://www.tamba.org.uk

Twins Trust
Twins Trust offer help, information and advice online and over the phone. They also run a unique service which helps families in desperate need.
https://twinstrust.org/

Tommys
Funds research into and support for miscarriage, stillbirth and premature birth and provides pregnancy health information to parents.
https://www.tommys.org

VBAC Support Group UK
This is a UK based support group for women in the UK planning to have a VBAC. They also offer support to women planning elective sections. (Facebook closed group)

PANDAS
Pandas is a community offering peer-to-peer support, hope and empathy for every parent or network affected by perinatal mental illness.
www.pandasfoundation.org.uk

Samaritans
Providing a confidential listening service.
https://www.samaritans.org

F.A.B (Families and Babies)
Offer evidence-based information and peer support on infant feeding to help improve health and wellbeing within families.
www.familiesandbabies.org.uk

Printed in Great Britain
by Amazon

52508807R00029